Neale Donald Walsch
on
HOLISTIC LIVING

Books by Neale Donald Walsch

Applications for Living

Neale Donald Walsch
on
HOLISTIC LIVING

Neale Donald Walsch

HAMPTON ROADS
PUBLISHING COMPANY, INC.

Cover design by Marjoram Productions
Cover art by Matthew and Jonathan Friedman

For information write:

Hampton Roads Publishing Company, Inc.
134 Burgess Lane
Charlottesville, VA 22902

Or call: 804-296-2772
FAX: 804-296-5096
e-mail: hrpc@hrpub.com
Web site: http://www.hrpub.com

If you are unable to order this book from your local
bookseller, you may order directly from the publisher.
Quantity discounts for organizations are available.
Call 1-800-766-8009, toll-free.

Library of Congress Catalog Card Number: 99-95398

ISBN 1-57174-165-8

10 9 8 7 6 5 4 3 2 1

Printed on acid-free paper in the United States

Dedication

To
Dennis Weaver

Actor, activist, friend, and partner on the path.

He honors the Divine in everyone.
He loves the Earth, and walks
with grace upon it.
He treats his body as a temple
of the Living Spirit.
He is a demonstration of what
holistic living is all about.

Introduction

What is it like to "walk the path"? What does living a whole—and a holy—life "look like"? Is there a way to take the messages of all the great spiritual literature and live it daily?

These are the questions all seekers ask. The answers have been given to us many times, in many different ways, from many different sources. Still, we are not living them. In the main, we are not paying attention to the words of those who would offer us spiritual guidance. The result is that we have lost our way. The *world* has lost *its* way. Yet we have no more time to act lost. Time is running out. For us, individually, and for the human family.

Each day that goes by is a day less that you will be here, in the body, on the Earth, doing what you came here to do. Are you clear what that is? And, is it what you are up to? Or, are you losing time, spending most of it still searching, still wandering, still wondering? If so, you are invited to stop it. The answers are here. They have been given us. All the great wisdom traditions contain them. And now they are more accessible than ever before. No longer are we dependent upon the passing of these truths through oral histories, or a few lost parchments finally found. Now we have mass media, and the World Wide Web. Now we have instant and global distribution of books and tapes and videos. If we are seekers today, we truly do not have to go far to find.

In truth, we never did. The answers were always right there, inside of us. That's the truth to which all this newly accessible information led me.

Like you, I'd been asking questions about how to live a better life for a long time. A few years ago, I began receiving answers. I believe those responses to have come from God. At the time I received them, I was so impacted and so impressed that I decided to keep a written record of what I was being given. That record became the *Conversations with God* series of books, which have become best-sellers around the world.

It is not necessary for you to join me in my belief about the source of my replies in order to receive benefit from them. All that is necessary is to remain open to the possibility that there just might be something that most humans do not fully understand about living holistically, the understanding of which could change everything.

That's the frame of mind that a small group of about forty people held when it gathered at a home just outside San Francisco, California, in January 1999 to explore with me more deeply what *Conversations with God* has to say on this subject. I shared with the group all that I understood about the material on holistic living that appears in the dialogue, and answered questions as they came up. The synergy of that afternoon produced an electrifying experience, resulting in an open flow of wonderful wisdom that, I am happy to say, was captured on videotape and audiocassette—edited versions of which have since been made public.

This book is a transcript of that event, and reads in a much more free-flowing—and, I think, more stimulating—style than text that is written for the printed page. And because the book format is not limited by time and production constraints, we were able to include here material not found in the video or audio versions, which necessarily had to be shortened for production reasons.

The guidance we are given here offers no surprises. As I've said, we have been given answers to life's most important questions before, in the Koran, in the Bhagavad Gita, in the Tao-te Ching, in the Bible, in the Dhammapada, in the Talmud, the Book of Mormon, the Upanishads, the Pali Canon, and in a hundred other places. The question is not, when we will be given the answers, but, when will we hear them?

It *is* possible to live life holistically, and the extraordinary insights in the *Conversations with God* books show us how. Again. In words just right for the twenty-first century.

Here are those insights, as I have received them and understood them. I share them with you here in humility, straight from the Take It for What It's Worth Department, with the hope that if even one comment opens a new window or throws wide a doorway to greater happiness you will have been served.

Neale Donald Walsch
July 1999
Ashland, Oregon

Holistic Living

Welcome to the room. Good to have you all here. We're going to talk today, together, about holistic living, what it's like to live as a whole person, and what stops us from living as whole people. We're going to take a look at why we see ourselves as separate—not only from each other, but even separate from within ourselves. And I want to begin by talking a bit about the aspect of our experience of life in this body that we call health.

I was at a place when I began my dialogue with God where my health had reached an all-time low. I mean, literally, my body was falling apart. I had arthritis at a level that was very, very painful a great deal of the time. I also had a very bad case of fibromyalgia. I had some heart difficulties that were continuing to plague me. One year in my life, I even had stomach ulcers. I mean, I just had a lot of stuff going on with my body. Today I feel healthier than I felt ten years ago. And I probably look a bit healthier, too, than I did ten years ago—although it wouldn't be hard. And so I wanted to just share with you what was given to me in my conversation with God about health.

The first thing that I was told was, I think, one of the most astonishing things I've ever been told about myself. "The difficulty, Neale, with you," God said to me, "is that you simply don't want to live."

And I said: "No, no, no. That's not true. Of course I want to live. What a strange and silly thing to say."

And God said: "No, no, you don't want to live; because if you wanted to live, you wouldn't be behaving the way you're behaving. I know that you think that you want to live, but you can't really want to live. And certainly it's clear that you do not want to live forever, and even forevermore. Because if you did, you wouldn't be doing the things that you're doing."

And I said, "Why, whatever do you mean?" And then God pointed out to me the things that I was doing that gave a signal to the universe that I really didn't care a whole lot about what happened to my body. I'm going to use one simple example, which may touch some of you in this room, unless it doesn't.

I used to smoke. And God said to me: "You cannot smoke and say that you really have a will to live. Because smoking kills you prematurely for sure."

In more than enough cases now—that doesn't have to be proven anymore. So, when you say, "I really have a will to live and want to live a long and vital life," and even as you're saying it, you're inhaling tobacco, you are really flying in the face of all the evidence that suggests that a long and fruitful life is not lived, at least not in the best way that we know how to live it, by doing this kind of thing to your body.

I just used a silly, simple example now. Or, for those of you who are eating extraordinary amounts of red meat . . . I want to say, all things in their proper balance. I know people who eat red meat at virtually every meal of their lives. In fact, they can't imagine a meal without it. And it's okay. There's nothing wrong with that. This is not about right and wrong. It's just about what works and what doesn't work within the framework of the human experience.

Some of our decisions about how we live our lives are not quite as clear-cut as that. They are not only about imbibing too much alcohol, or partaking of hallucinogenic drugs, something as obviously detrimental to us as that. Sometimes they have to do with something much more subtle. A kind of mental diet, or mental ingestion of ideas and thoughts that do not serve us, and do not allow us to maintain healthy lives.

For instance, I found out in my conversations with God that anything other than a totally positive attitude in life can create disease. I was made aware that even the smallest negativities, repeated over, and over, and over again, indulged in over and over again, will ultimately produce an effect inside the human body, that we will call illness or disease. And I was astonished with the number of times in my life where I found myself being less than positive in my thoughts. Little thoughts like, "Well, I can never win," or "That will never happen for me," or larger negative thoughts.

And so I learned to begin to control the thoughts that I allow to reside in my mind, so that I wouldn't be surrounded by the negative energies that they attract to me. This is particularly true about my thoughts regarding other people.

When I was a younger man, I not only found myself with great dislikes toward certain people, but, to be really honest with you (I'm very transparent), I allowed myself even to *entertain* such thoughts. I mean, at some level, they even made me feel good.

You know, that's hard to admit, but there was a part of me that just reveled in the anger that I felt toward some people, or the dislike that I allowed myself to experience with regard to certain people. And that anger, and that dislike, which fed a certain part of me, I didn't realize until recently was feeding that part of me with very damaging stuff.

People who are angry, you know—even a little bit, but consistently so—find themselves having heart attacks, find themselves having stomach troubles, find themselves having ulcers, find themselves experiencing negative physical conditions.

Or, to put it another way, I know of very, very few people who are eternally cheerful who are always ill. I suppose there is the exception that proves the rule, but I have to tell you that, in the main, you find that the degree of positivity with which one moves through life is almost always directly in concert or in harmony with the degree to which one expresses and exhibits the experience of healthfulness. And conversely, we find that people who are largely unhealthy, who are constantly having bouts with this, that, or the other, who have chronic illnesses and diseases, are often people who, to some degree or another, have allowed themselves to entertain negative thoughts about life, and have surrounded themselves with negative energies.

Chief among these negative energies is the energy that I want to call (again I use the word) anger, and a new word that I'll add to that, resentment. I'm talking about people who are resentful of others for roles that they have played in their lives prior to now. And people who live in the present moment carrying the pain of those former days and times as if they were happening right here, right now.

I mean, you can sometimes look at somebody, and on a scale of one to ten, you can almost measure the amount of pain that they're carrying around with them. Pain that, no doubt to them—not to make it wrong—no doubt is very real. But also pain that is no longer serving them, and has very little to do with here and now, but has to do with there and then. And these are people who will simply not, because they think that they can't (not that they don't want to, but they absolutely have themselves convinced that they can't), let go of it.

"Neale, you don't understand; you just don't understand. If what happened to me, happened to you, then you'd understand. But you clearly don't understand." And they won't really allow anyone to take that pain from them, even if they could. Because if they let go of that pain, then they'd be letting go of all of their drama and all of the stuff that justifies the way they are and the way they've been for all these many years. Even though in some cases, it's been eight, ten, fifteen, twenty, thirty years since the original injury or damaging experience occurred.

But to hang on to that, and to make that part of their living reality, through all those days and times, does nothing, of course, but allow the person who did that original damage to continue doing the damage for thirty years—and to do it over, and over, and over again.

As I said, we've all known people like this, and sometimes, you know, your heart goes out to them. And you say: "What can I do? How can I assist you in noticing that 'that was then, and this is now,' and that you don't have to hang onto that?"

I can tell you that nothing damages the human mechanism, the human organism, this biological house that we're in, faster or more profoundly than those kinds of unresolved negative thoughts or emotions that we're carrying around with us from some "yester-moment" that we think has pretty much decided for us who and what we are, and who and what we are going to be.

So, one of the first steps in holistic living is forgiveness. And I mean that in two ways. Life is not for getting, but it is for giving. And until we've learned the divine healing, until we've used the balm of forgiveness on our wounds, those wounds will fester inside of us long after the outward scars have apparently disappeared. And we will find ourselves, at 36, or 42, or 51, or 63, undergoing enormous physiological challenges and we won't know where they came from.

I read a story in the paper just yesterday on the plane on the way out here of a 41-year-old man who died in New York City of a heart attack. And his girlfriend was calling 911, and she couldn't get anyone to answer, because the system was down for an hour. And he left his body for good. But I thought . . . by all reckoning, all those who knew him, a very healthy guy, 41 years old. Just left. But there was obviously stuff going on inside of him.

One of the teachings of my conversations with God, and one of the most difficult things I've had to deal with, in absorbing and accepting this material, is the statement: *All illness is self-created.* Now, that's difficult, because people then want to go to another favorite place of ours, which is the place of self-flagellation and guilt, as in "Why am I doing this to myself?" As a matter of fact, if there's anything I hate more, I don't know what it is—a person who walks up to you with an attitude when you have an illness or a sickness, and says to you, "Why are you doing that to yourself?" I tell them: Thank you for sharing. And then I mutter something about the horse they rode in on.

There may be a seed of wisdom, though I don't think the confrontation is very useful. But we might ask ourselves indeed, "Why am I creating that?" But, more importantly and much more to the point, "What would it take for me now to step away from this?" So know that all illness is, at some level, self-created. And once we understand that, we'll understand that even what we would call, I guess, the greatest illness of all, which would be labeled in our experience "death," is also self-created.

I was told, actually, that we don't really have to die, but that all of us have elected, for various sundry reasons, to ultimately leave our physical body. Because, frankly, we're through with it, and we no longer need this particular life and this particular form to achieve and to accomplish what we came here to achieve and to accomplish. Masters who know and understand this leave their bodies very gracefully, just like you take off a piece of clothing you no longer find useful, or step away from any experience that no longer serves you. So masters simply step away from their current bodily form, and say: "So be it, that is the end of that. And now on to the next grand adventure, and the next glorious expression of who I really am."

There's a level of detachment, or dis-attachment, if you will, from that particular physical form. But while we are holding that form, and while it pleases us to do so, how nice to be able to hold that form from a place of health, and vibrancy, and wonderment in the expression of who we really are. And it is possible to do that by simply obeying some very, very simple rules, the physiological health rules we all know about. Yet there are many of us who simply find it impossible to obey those rules. So the first thing that God said to me in the chapter of *Conversations with God* on health was: "For heaven's sake, take better care of yourself. I mean, you're taking better care of your car than you are of your body. And that's not saying much, by the way.

"You take your car in for checkups more than you take your body in for checkups. And you change the oil in your car more than you change some of your habits, and some of the things you're putting into your body. So, for heaven's sake, take better care of your body."

I just want to give you some very simple, if not to say simplistic, formulas.

Number one, exercise. Do something with your body every day that allows it to feel used and exercised, even just a bit. It's amazing what fifteen or twenty minutes a day (which is not a lot) can do for the human body.

Second, watch what it is that you are putting into your body. Look to see whether it serves you to keep on putting in so much junk. Just completely cut out, for the most part—well, almost—the junk that you're putting into your body, the stuff that just doesn't serve it to be in there. I'm not talking about the obvious stuff: the sugars, the sweets, most of the carbos, and those things that clearly aren't doing us a whole lot of good. I've lost a great deal of weight, in fact, in the past several months, as a result of these new ideas I have about what it serves me to ingest. And so now,

I'm a little bit trim and slim, at least compared to where I was a year ago.

Now, it isn't that thin is better, or heavy is not so good. That's not the point. If you feel good at your present weight, then terrific, that's fine. But if you don't feel good at your present weight, if you're starting to walk around a little bit sluggishly, and you don't feel like you're operating at your optimum level, then you may want to take some very simple, simple precautions. So take some simple steps to allow yourselves to maintain a higher level of health—exercise, and watching your diet, of course, are the obvious ones, and then, as I said, watching that mental diet as well.

But holistically, it only begins there. It just starts at that rather simplistic level. Holistic living, however, ends, and moves into and toward an expression of the self that is whole and complete. And then one is said to live a holy life. That means that we operate at all three levels of creation, and from the seven energy levels that we have come to call the chakras of the human bodily system. And holistic living suggests that we don't abandon any of those chakra experiences, or deny any of those energies that flow through us.

Let me talk specifically about the energy that we call the human sexual energy, because a lot has been said about how one lives a holistic life, and how one lives a spiritual life.

Some people have suggested that a highly spiritual life requires us to be what you and I would call celibate, or nonsexual, or asexual, if you please—that we would deny our sexual energy. And that people who are overtly sexual, who revel and find great joy in the expression of their human sexuality, are okay, not like bad or wrong, but they're just not really very highly evolved. One day they'll get there, and one day get it, but in the meantime, they're doing what they're doing.

There's a whole school of thought that suggests that holy people have little or nothing to do with sex. As a matter of fact, this school of thought runs rampant through some traditions to such a degree that you are required to denounce and refuse to experience your sexuality

in order to call yourself a member of that culture or that sub-strata of the culture.

I asked God about this, because this is
something I wanted to know about. I said,
"God, is it true that in order for me to live a really holistic life, and to experience and express
the grandest part of who I am, that I must really,
really deny the . . . " (and I want to say I almost
put it like this) "the lowest part of who I am?"
And I don't mean even the lowest part in terms
of the lowest chakra. I mean the lowest part in
terms of the mind-set that I held about it.

It seemed that of all the aspects of myself,
this thing I called my sexuality was the lowest
aspect. It was an aspect of my being that I was
willing to own, but not terribly openly, not very
overtly, and not very proudly, except in certain
circumstances and in certain moments of my
life. And so, I had this shame about it, this level
of embarrassment. I have had that experience
profoundly in my life, where I was embarrassed
and ashamed, and I had been made to feel, as a
child, that my social expression was something
of which I should at least be circumspect, if not

ashamed. In fact, I remember once, I was in the early stages of puberty, perhaps twelve or thirteen, maybe just a bit younger, and I was drawing some pictures of women, copying pictures out of a magazine, and just reveling in the, you know, the wonderful curves . . . and just the wonderful little stimulation of that. You know how you do when you're twelve, and you're just kind of being what you want to call—here's a clue, by the way—a little bit naughty. Whatever is naughty about that. But I recall doing this.

And my mom came into the room. And she happened to catch me drawing these pictures of naked ladies. I loved my mother, of course. She was a wonderful person. She's no longer in the body. But I remember the moment well, because I was very, very embarrassed. Because her first reaction was one of being utterly aghast that her son was drawing these naked ladies on this tablet.

She said, "What are you doing?" And the general sense of it was that this was probably something with which I ought not be occupying my mind. And, of course, it was *all* that was occupying my mind during that period in my life ... and for a number of years thereafter, actually. As I recall ... even to this present day—to some degree ...

And these days, I can enjoy that. These days, I can laugh and find joy in that part of myself that can admit and acknowledge that I find it still delightful to contemplate the human form, and particularly the human form of a gender opposite of my own. In particular cases, that's where my stimulation lies. That doesn't make it right or wrong. It's just what it is for me.

But it took me the largest part of a half century—imagine that—to go to a place where I didn't feel that, by announcing that, I was declaring that I was somehow less evolved, perhaps a bit less spiritual, perhaps a bit less something or other. And that had to do with many, many episodes—like that moment when my mother caught me red-handed, as it were, drawing these pictures at the age of twelve—a whole slew of those kinds of experiences, in which society allowed me to notice that it was definitely a no-no, that really evolved people didn't have those kinds of experiences.

And it had more to do with than just childish inappropriateness, although there was nothing inappropriate at all about what I was doing. But it had to do with more than just that. It had to do with our adult notions (and I'm going to circle back on this) of what it really is to be evolved and holy; that people who are really in a holy place simply don't engage those energies, and have those kinds of experiences. Well, they do. And perhaps that is what *makes* them holy.

So, when I moved into my conversation with God, I asked the question: "What about this lower chakra energy stuff? Do I have to release that whole experience of myself and just let it go, in order to evolve?" I'd heard all these stories about how you must raise the energy, raise the energy—up from the root chakra, through the power chakra, through the heart chakra, into the crown chakra. And then you're living in this wonderful place. And you have nothing to do with anything below your neck. That's how it is for real masters. Real masters don't live below their neck. From the neck up, I am such a master.

And I always wondered: "How can that be? Is that the way God really wanted it for us? There's got to be something more than that." And then I learned about how, yes, God says for us to live a holistic life, that we live through all of the energy or chakra centers of the body. We engage fully the root chakra, fully the power of chakra. We engage fully the heart chakra. We engage fully the highest chakra of all. We engage fully all of our chakras.

But once we get up here, it's not about getting up here, then letting the bottom five go. See, it's not about cutting it off. But rather it's about . . . I didn't mean cutting that off, in particular—not what I was talking about. And I don't know what you're laughing at. She kind of winced when I said that. I think she has the wrong idea of what I'm discussing here. It's not about, it's not about separating yourself from the . . . stay with me. It's not about separating yourself from those five lower chakras. And just residing in those upper, or in this last one. That isn't what's happening. It's about really bringing that energy up, but also maintaining your connection with all the chakras beneath it. And then you live holistically.

Living a holistic life involves more than even this—more than even purifying your thoughts, or getting rid of negativity; more than some of the simplistic solutions of living healthfully and watching your diet; more than even living from all of your chakra centers, from the whole part of you.

It involves recontextualizing your whole life, and coming to some new understandings about how the whole thing works. I mean, the whole process that we call life itself. And it involves coming to new clarity about the wholeness of who you are, who you really are. Most people are finding it very difficult, in these days and time—and have really from the beginning of time—to live their life from the largest idea of the wholeness of who they really are. And the reason they have difficulty with that is because they're caught in fear. Most people's lives, to one degree or another, are run by fear.

Conversations with God tells us that there are only two places from which every thought, word, or deed springs; that everything we think, say, and do has its origin in either love or fear. And for a great many members of the human race, a great deal of the time, it's fear that controls and creates the thought, the word, and the deed. And so one of our first steps toward moving into wholeness and toward living a holistic life is the step away from fear. You know, the acronym for fear is "false evidence appearing real." There's another acronym, which is "feeling excited and ready."

One of my great teachers shared that with me one day, and said this sentence to me, which I've never forgotten: "Neale, call your fears adventure." Isn't that a great thing to say? Call your fears adventure. When I began to do that, I began to step away from my fear. I also began to look at what it was that I ultimately was afraid of. And, of course, what I was ultimately afraid of, at the end of the line, was God. See, I thought that God would never forgive me for all the things that I was or all the things that I was not; for the times that I failed to live up to what I thought was God's idea about who I should be; or for all the times when I behaved in a way that was inappropriate, according to what I imagined God's requirements to be.

And, oh, those requirements have been laid upon me by every segment of my society, and by many, many people in my life. And only when I began to create and to experience my own personal relationship with God could I step away from my fear of God's reaction to the way I've lived my life.

Here is the statement that God would have all of us make, even as we review our litany of supposed offenses: "I am guiltless, and I am innocent. I am guiltless, and I am innocent."

That doesn't mean that I've never done anything in my life that I wouldn't do over again a different way. It doesn't even mean that I choose to stand away from a place of responsibility for the outcomes that I helped to co-create. It means, however, that I am guilt-less, and I am innocent of any crime.

If being human is a crime, then I'm guilty. If being an evolving entity is a crime, then I am guilty. If growing in awareness, in sensitivity, in understanding in the expression of who I am is a crime, then I'm guilty. But if those things are not crimes, and I assure you in the kingdom of God they are not, then I am guiltless, and I am innocent. And God is not going to punish me because somehow I didn't get it right. And least of all, *least of all*, will God punish me because I haven't done it the way *someone else* said was right.

Well, I'll just share with you a personal experience from my childhood. Remember I was born and raised a Roman Catholic, and I was taught at an early age, of course, to make the sign of the cross, which is a uniquely Catholic (although not necessarily Roman Catholic) thing to do. The Greek Orthodox make the sign of the cross as well.

Now, here's what I remember being taught. The sign of the cross, with no disrespect meant to anyone please—don't anyone get nervous about this—was done like this: "In the name of the Father, and of the Son, and of the Holy Spirit." [motions] Now, the Greek Orthodox, if I have this correctly—if there's a Greek Orthodox in the audience, then I'm sure you'll tell me—do it like this. [motions]

Did you notice anything different? I touched this shoulder first, and then went to this one, rather than the other way around. I remember in third grade the nun telling me that this way was wrong, and it didn't work—or at least that was the inference that my third-grade mind got from what she said was the wrong way to make the sign of the cross.

Now, there are a lot of wrong ways to do all sorts of things, you know. There are people that say you have to spread out a carpet and bow to the East at least three times a day. There are people that say that you are supposed to only stand before one particular portion of the Wailing Wall. And if you're a woman, you can't stand with the men. There are people who say that you have to do this particular ritual and that particular ritual, or you cannot go to heaven. And so we've been filled with these ideas and concepts about what is right and wrong, and what God requires and does not require. And it is remarkable the amount of guilt that we carry with us for the things we have done in our lives. Some of which were really the innocent, pure actings-out of childhood. And that's the saddest thing of all, when even a little child is made to feel guilty about something they've done.

I remember when I was around eleven years old or so that I was having a hamburger, and I suddenly realized, "Oh, my God, it's Friday." I was a very devout, young Catholic boy, and so I thought I had committed a sin, because I had been told that eating meat on Fridays was, in fact, a venial sin. And I remember I was very nervous, because I had done this, and forgot myself for a minute.

My mother took a look at me when I came into the house. I had gotten it at the local fast-food joint. And she said: "What's the matter? Are you okay? Did somebody beat you up?

What happened?" And I said: "No, but I ate meat, I ate meat. I forgot it was Friday. God is going to be mad at me." That's what I really, really thought, in my eleven-year-old mind. My heart was breaking that I did this thing, because I was very devout—I was even an altar boy, if you can imagine. What are you laughing at?

And so, I said to my mother: "I had meat. I forgot it was Friday." My mother, God bless her, she just held me in her arms, and she said: "Sweetheart, it's okay. I'm sure it's all right. Don't be upset about it."

Now, my mother was wise enough to know that at the age of eleven, I probably wasn't ready to hear that God simply didn't care. Only years later, when I turned twenty-one, could I even begin to grasp that thought. Because at the age of twenty-one, as it happened, a huge headline found its way to the top of the page of our local paper. And it said, "Pope declares eating meat on Friday no longer a sin." And I thought to myself, "Isn't that wonderful! Now, all those people who ate meat on Fridays can get out of . . ." They never went to hell, of course, because they wouldn't go to hell for eating meat. It was simply purgatory, because, eating meat on Fridays was kind of a moral misdemeanor, but it wasn't really a huge crime.

I can take my own particular upbringing, and I hope that you'll give me leave because I speak from my own childhood. All of us can tell stories like that about how we were allowed, whatever our religious background, to be, or made to feel, guilty about those kinds of things.

Well, I have to tell you that if it was just limited to small stuff like that (what my father would call "small potatoes"), it would not be a problem. But the truth is, half the human race is carrying huge guilt about enormous stuff that are simply expressions of the wonder of who we are, such as, to touch on the earlier subject, the joyful and celebratory expression of our own sexuality, to name an obvious example of some of the things we've been allowing ourselves to feel guilty about. Or, for that matter, having a lot of money—some people feel very guilty about having a great deal of money. They allow themselves to feel so guilty, they start giving it away like crazy in order to assuage their guilt. "Yeah, I have a lot of money, but I give away a quarter-million dollars a year. I can feel a little bit better about this horrible thing that's happened to me."

And you especially shouldn't have a lot of money if you're teaching the word of God, or doing something else that's really wonderful. So we pay our teachers nothing; we pay our nurses next to nothing. The more valuable a thing is to society, the less we pay. What does that tell you about how guilty we are about any of the good stuff in life, much less about the honest—what I want to call human—mistakes that we make, the errors in judgment, and I mean errors only in the sense that we ourselves wouldn't do it twice, wouldn't do it again?

We beat ourselves up, and self-flagellate, and make ourselves so wrong that if we're not careful, we even create our own hell on Earth as a result of the mistakes that we've made, and in that way, as well, bring ourselves disease, and fail to live a holistic life.

So one of the grandest, most free-dom-giving, most releasing statements you can ever hope to make is: "I am guiltless and inno-cent." And then come from that place of pureness, that place of wonder, that place of wholeness. Because you can put yourself back together again, like Humpty Dumpty, once you accept your guiltlessness.

Remember what I said earlier in our shar-ing: Forgiveness is the key to wholeness. And now I add an addendum: Forgiveness that starts right here. And in fact, unless the forgiveness starts here, it can't go anywhere. Because you cannot give what you do not have.

Holistic living means living with all of it, the whole of it, the up and the down of it, the left and the right of it, the here and the there, the before and the after, the male and the fe-male of it. All of us have that male and female energy running through us—in, as, and through us. It means disowning none of it, yet simply owning it all, then releasing that which no lon-ger serves us, which no longer makes the highest statement of who we imagine ourselves to be, and then hanging on to the rest, even as we give it away, freely and openly, to all those lives we touch.

> *Some of the people are going to be bringing up small children. What advice do you have for parents these days? What can we tell them? How can we teach them about God?*

You know the danger of sitting in this chair is imagining that I have an answer for all of these questions. I'm the last person to ask for advice for parents. I'm probably on the top ten list of the world's worst parents. Maybe that makes me a good person to ask, I don't know. I can tell you all the mistakes that I've made. I think, however, that there's one mistake I haven't made. I've never failed to love my children without condition. And to ask nothing of them that I didn't think they wanted to give . . . to me or to life. So I guess the advice I would give to parents is, love them as you would like to be loved. Don't come from expectation.

Don't come from any requirement, and most of all, allow them to live their lives.

Release them. Let them go. Let them walk into those walls and make those mistakes. Let them hurt themselves now and then. Pick them up and help them if you can when they have a little owie. But don't try to stop them from living their lives. Give them their freedom—even freedom to do something that's clearly not in their best interests, and that you might even call "wrong."

You know, the best advice I could give to parents is to treat your children as God treats us: "Your will for you is my will for you. I give you free choice to make the decisions in life that you wish to make, and I will never stop loving you, no matter what." I wish I had had that with my own parents. I wish I had done that with my own children. I wish I had that kind of relationship, I mean. But we try.

I think the other thing I would say to parents is, don't forget you're a parent. I mean, much of my life I'd really forgotten that I was a parent. In that way I emotionally deserted my children. That's profoundly not okay.

Any words on the subject of love?

I think love is the most misunderstood emotion in the universe. I don't think half the people know what real love is. And I don't think that half the people on this planet have ever experienced it. If people experienced for one moment what real love is, we could never live the way we live with each other. We couldn't do to each other what we're doing. We couldn't ignore what we're ignoring. We couldn't allow it to be the way it is.

The first problem, of course, is that we haven't learned to love ourselves. That's the first problem. We can only give to another what we have to give. And if we have no love over here, we can't give it over there. These are obvious things to say . . . it's embarrassing to say them, they're so obvious.

What is the final word I would say about love? Try it some time. But if you're going to try it, try it full out. Full out! Try to love someone just once, just one person without any condition or limitation of any kind. With no expectation, with nothing required in return. Just try, just once, to love someone like that. But be careful, because if you do it once, and you feel that feeling, you'll be addicted.

Now, I thought I'd ask the room, because this is a huge subject I'm really trying to button down into a small segment, for any questions, because now is your time, now is your chance to ask any questions you might have at all. Here is the first question right here.

> *What do you say to people regarding their genes? Everything from being overweight, to cancer . . . Some people feel that they're destined to have cancer based on their past family genetic makeup. What do you say to those people who say that there's no control? It just happens.*

As you believe, and as you speak, so will it be done unto you. And there is ample evidence in the annals of medical history of people who have absolutely moved against the grain, if you please, and produced outcomes exactly to the contrary of what their genetic makeup ought to have produced, where genetics, in fact, should have been the controlling factor.

I think it would be foolhardy to suggest that there's no such thing as genetic predisposition. Science has demonstrated otherwise convincingly. And so a genetic predisposition toward a particular condition, for instance, is a reality. But it does not have to be a condition from which there is no escape. It doesn't have to be an inevitability.

Because one has a predisposition toward a certain condition does not mean that we have no control over that. If there were absolutely no control that we could have over our predispositions, mentally, physically, psychologically, we would be said to have predestination; we'd be subject to the whims of fate, as it were— physiological fate, if nothing else. And that simply isn't the condition of the human experience.

Many of our predispositions have been chosen—I mean programmed in. There's a school of thought that says that no one comes into a particular body by mistake. And so it might be said that some of the predispositions that are built into the biomechanical system that we call our body are conditions that we have chosen ahead of time, that we really have selected as tools with which to work, as colors, or brushes with which to paint on the canvas of our life. But we can change those colors any time we want. I mean really, in mid-painting. We could say: "No, I've got too much blue. I think I'm going to go with orange." And we can produce a new canvas, or a new look on the original one.

And so, I think it's important for us to understand that there is no aspect of the human life experience that's more powerful than our idea about it, than our decision and our choice about it, and that nothing is large enough to overcome our co-creative partnership with God.

If God and I decide to change something in the biochemical factory called my body, we'll go ahead and do that, predisposition or not. And, really, nothing can stop that process. And it is precisely *by* this process that people have cured themselves of cancer, and turned around other physical and emotional conditions by which they might otherwise have been beset, and imagined themselves to have been fated to experience.

The genes of your body are simply indicators, not unlike astrology, astrological signs. I think that the genes in our body provide us signs, much like astrological signs are provided for the largest body that we call the universe. And so each of us, it's been said, is a universe in miniature. And I think our genes are not unlike astrological signs. That is to say, they can be indicators of directions in which we may travel, but they are not signs of the inevitable. And so our genes simply point the way, indicate a path that could be taken and that, in fact, is most likely to be taken, if you please, unless we change our mind about that.

And if we don't like what our genes are telling us about the direction in which we may go physiologically, we must change our mind about it. It is precisely by this process of changing our mind about the directions in which our genes are sending us that people have overcome so called nonovercomeable conditions—cancer among them, and many others. So we can change our mind whenever we want, and produce a new experience. However, and this is what's critical, not very many people actually believe that. And because very few people believe it, very few people have demonstrated it.

Is it possible for us to overcome either our genetic background or any other environmental condition that should be producing certain outcomes or experiences for us? If it is not, if it is not possible, then the grandest promise of God is a lie, and you do not have free will, and you are not in charge of your own destiny. And we've been told an extraordinary untruth. But I don't believe that. The evidence of my eyes, and the evidence of my life, demonstrates the contrary . . .

Even before you wrote the three books, and in between each of the books, were you in touch with having conversations with God? In what form did they take?

Before the books became books, before the material came through me, I was not consciously aware of having what we now call conversations with God. No. Only after the material came through—which, by the way, did not come through in the form of a book . . . it was really in the form of a very private dialogue that I was having with myself. But only after that experience began did I become aware.

From that time on, I have been keenly aware that my whole life, and yours as well—is a conversation with God. And that all of us not only *may* have conversations with God, but are having them every day.

One of the questions I'm most frequently asked is, "Why you?" The answer is, it isn't me. I'm not the chosen one. In fact, all of us are having conversations with God every day of our lives. We're simply not knowing it, or not calling them that.

And so, would you begin to see your life, lived, as your conversation with God? When you hear your conversation with God, in the form of the lyrics of the next song that is on the radio, or the storyline of the next novel you happen to pick up, or the material in the next magazine article that you find in the barbershop, or the chance utterance of a friend on the street, or, indeed, in the form of words that are whispered in your right ear, will you hear and experience all of that as your own personal conversation with God? Then you will have the experience that you ask me about, and that you think that I am the only one who could have.

The important thing to know about conversations with God is that there are some easy steps to follow, should you choose to have those kinds of conversations as part of your reality.

The first step is to openly announce and declare to yourself that it's even possible. How many of you really believe that God can and will talk to you directly on this day of your life?

Good. Terrific. Almost all of you in this room. That's great. Because that's the first step—to actually say, "Wait a minute, this is possible, this can be, and in fact is, happening right now."

The second step, after acknowledging the possibility of it, is to allow yourself to believe that you are worthy to be one of those who is able to experience that. We are all able, but very few of us can acknowledge our worthiness. Self-worth is a huge, huge issue among many people, for a lot of the reasons I've talked about in the earlier part of our conversation here.

Much of what we've been taught mitigates against our sense of self-worth, and causes us to feel worth less, worth less than we thought we ought to be worth, so we wind up feeling worthless. And if you think that the feeling of worthlessness is uncommon among people, think again. Many people move through their lives feeling worthless. And so step number two in having your own conversation with God is moving into and accepting as a fact that you are worth it, that you are worthy of such a conversation.

And the third step is, once you acknowledge your worthiness, to notice that the conversation is going on, as I said, all the time. And to stop writing it off as something else, as though it's just a coincidence. Just a coincidence? Let's say I've been worried about this problem for the last few weeks, and I walk into the beauty shop. There's a magazine—for three-and-a-half months it's been sitting there. And I pick it up, and there's this sixteen-page article on the very subject I've been concerned about. What's that about?

I can't tell you how many people have written me letters, saying that this *CWG* fell off the shelf into their hands, or came to them by some other serendipitous route. And you couldn't even believe, I can't tell you how many letters we've received from people who have said: "This book came to me at just the right moment of my life." What's that about? Only when you are deeply aware of how that process has taken place can you begin to understand that this is all part of your own conversation.

But the most important part of the conversation, which we are all capable of having, and which you are all having every day, is not so much what you imagine, understand, or hear God to be saying to you, but what *you* are saying to *God*. And again, I want to say that your end of the conversation with God is your life, lived. The thoughts that you think moment to moment, the words that you speak, the things that you do—this is your conversation. And there is none other. So be careful that you do not say one thing and do another, or think one thing and say another. But have your thoughts, your words, and your deeds all in alignment, so that you are thinking what you are saying what you are doing. And then your conversation will be holy indeed. That is to say, it will be whole. And your life will be holistic.

You have a question?

In the process of bringing that kind of alignment that you were just speaking about into our own lives, could you speak more about what you talked about in Book 3, *how our technology and our consciousness are at such odds with each other, and what our course for the future is going to be?*

Yes. We're at a real crossroads right now. We're at a time, and we've come to this crossroads before, where technology is threatening us, and probably is at this point exceeding our understanding of how to use it. At least, that's true of a great many people, almost too many people at this point, unless we turn things around very quickly. You see, we're also at another point that's fascinating in the evolution of the human species. We are at a point of what Barbara Marx Hubbard called *conscious evolution.* Let me explain.

Until these most recent days and times, the process that we call evolution (the evolution of the species) seemed to be a process that we were, by and large, observing. We were watching our evolution take place right before our eyes. We were seeing the thing happen. Sometimes we did so with, you know, with bemusement. Like I can't believe this. Sometimes we did so with gratitude and excitement. But mostly, we thought of ourselves as watching the process take place around us. It was recorded in history books, and we can read about past evolutionary advances in those books, and so forth.

Only recently, relatively recently, not even throughout the entirety of some of our lives here, but only relatively recently, say, in the past twenty, thirty, or forty years, have we become consciously aware not only of the process of evolution, but of the part that we're playing in it.

Only relatively recently have we become aware that we are *creating* the way in which we are evolving. That's a new level of awareness for most members of the species. And so now we are engaged in a new process called conscious evolution. That is to say, we are beginning to *direct the course and the way* in which we are, as a species, and as individuals, evolving.

This represents a huge shift in the way evolution takes place. You see? It couldn't come at a better time. Because it also happens to be coincident with the time in which our technology is threatening to overcome our ability to use it wisely. For we haven't even yet defined what "wisely" is.

We talk about such moral dilemmas as cloning, just to use one example, or genetic engineering, to use another. And there are hundreds of them—ways in which our society has created technology that we haven't begun to learn how to use yet. And some technology that is extremely dangerous to our health, to our environment (which is the same thing), and to the way in which we choose to live as *Homo sapiens* on the planet.

So, we need now to take a look at this race against time, and to consciously choose how we seek to evolve with regard to the technologies that have heretofore been driving the engine of our experience. To which technologies do we wish to say: "Just a cotton-picking minute. Just a moment. I don't think so." Can we say yes to this, and no to that? Can we make wise choices and decisions? And can we apply the highest thoughts we hold in common about who we really are, as an overlay on the technological advances and applications that our society permits, allows, creates, encourages, and experiences?

This is the most pressing question, really, of our time. It's not a small question. And those of you in this room, and others like you everywhere, are being called now to the front line of that inquiry.

This is not a question that will be answered by someone else, some place else, but a question that you will answer. You will answer the question by the products you consume, the individual choices that you make at the supermarket, in the clothing store, on the street where you live.

You will answer these questions in your everyday lives: in what you say to others, in how you encourage others, in what you choose, in the choices that you share, and how you share them. And unless you're really deeply aware of what I'm saying to you, and the implications of what I've just said, you may just write this off as just so much talk.

I encourage you to read an extraordinary book called *The Last Hours of Ancient Sunlight,* by Thom Hartmann. While you're at it, do read Barbara Marx Hubbard's book, *Conscious Evolution.* And if I can work in a third and final one, do not fail to read Marianne Williamson's *Healing the Soul of America.* These books address this topic very specifically, very dynamically . . . with great articulation, and with wondrous insight.

But give yourself permission to at least move to the level of awareness that the question invites; an awareness that we are at the precipice now, as we move into the twenty-first century and beyond. We are in a race against time. Who will win?

Technology or the human spirit? Technology won once before, and virtually obliterated human life on this planet—all but eliminated it. And we, of course, have the ability to do that again. I want to tell you it's probably not going to happen. We all were afraid it was going to happen in the fifties. I don't get that it's going to be one big explosion, and that Manhattan will be destroyed, or that Moscow will be disintegrated by some atom bomb or something. That could happen, but I don't think that's the way it would happen, if it's going to happen. It will be insidious things, that seem to take a lifetime to produce results, with which we will not want to live.

So, I think it's very important for us to begin to pay attention to these slow, but sure, eradications of the quality of our life. You know, let's stop chopping down the rain forests. Can we agree on that? It's really relatively simple. And let's start finding a way that we can feed everyone, so we don't have four hundred children dying on this planet every single hour.

Question?

Neale, from a holistic health standpoint, what do you think we can do to nurture mind, body, and spirit . . . keep it all in balance?

I think that a real challenge in this day and time is to nurture mind, body, and spirit, simultaneously, and to keep ourselves in balance.

That's very difficult in a world that is so out of whack that it often seems out of balance to us. And because the world seems out of balance, we tend to go out of balance with it, as kind of a compensating mechanism: we go out of balance the other way.

For instance, if we're deeply engaged in a spiritual process over a long period of time, say, in a spiritual community, we may go out of balance and start getting very much into our bodies, forgetting altogether that we're spiritual beings. And likewise, if we're deeply involved in a very physical kind of life, which is not receiving a lot of spiritual nourishment, sometimes people do intensive retreats or workshops and seminars, and they go so deeply into the spiritual aspect of their beingness, that they really can't pull out of it. And they wind up riding on a workshop high for six or eight months that bears, really, no resemblance to day-to-day reality, and the reality in which they are living. So the real challenge is to achieve a place of balance. I think it was Gerald

Jampolsky who said, "Life is a question of balance."

And the way to achieve that balance is to remember that we are three-part beings, and that no part of our three-part being is more important, or more sacred, than any other part. We are, in fact, body, mind, and spirit.

There are some people who like to suggest that it is the spiritual part of us, our spirit, that is the most sacred, and therefore the most important. That would not be accurate. The spiritual part of who you are is no more important, and should be nurtured no more, than the physical or the mental part of you.

And yet, of course, the reverse can also be said. We don't pay enough attention to our bodies. I've said this before. We're not exercising our bodies. We're not keeping our bodies in shape. We're not keeping our bodies well toned. We're paying, really, precious little attention to our bodies in largest measure. That's true for most people. And as a result, particularly in the United States, people tend to be largely overweight, and out of condition. And they die much sooner than they should, because of these and other physical conditions to which they have paid scarce attention.

We also don't pay nearly enough attention to the nurturing of our minds. I'm amazed how few books people read in the average year. I've taken to asking that question of people wherever I go. "How many books have you read in the last year?" If they say three or four, it starts to sound like a lot. You know, I read twenty or thirty, and sometimes fifty, almost a book a week when I'm really voracious. This isn't about bragging, but it's about noticing. I thought that was the average. I thought that's how it was for most people. But if a guy reads three or four books a year, he feels very proud of himself.

The largest way that we nurture our minds, for most people, I regret to say, is turning on the television set. Or maybe going out to see a movie, if you call that nurturing the mind. But the last time the average person went to a library and sat there on a Sunday afternoon to see what Balzac had to say about anything—most people have never done that in their entire lives—in their *entire lives*. And their minds are starving for something other than the Simpsons, or the sports pages of the *Los Angeles Times*.

Most people do not nurture their spiritual side, either. They don't meditate. Very few people spend time nurturing the spiritual aspect of themselves in other ways. They don't go to church or synagogue or to a place of worship as regularly as they might, and some, not at all. They don't pay attention to the fact that they are one-third, if you please, spirit. I mean, we're all spirit, but we're three-part beings. And they don't pay 33 percent of their time and attention to the spiritual side of themselves. But most of us nurture one area over the other, rather than all three equally.

Any suggestion on how they can change that?

Stop doing that. The way to change all that is to notice that we are three-part beings, and begin to be deliberately attentive to every aspect of yourself, even if it makes you uncomfortable to do so. Move past the edge of your comfort zone.

For those of you who feel uncomfortable in a church or synagogue or spiritual setting or doing meditation, do it anyway. By the way, that's how I began meditation. I was never really terribly comfortable with the idea of sitting down for an hour with a candle or some soft music or in the dead of night, just being quiet with myself. But because I wasn't comfortable with the idea and didn't think, frankly, I even had the stamina to sit there quietly for an hour, I tried it. And I tried it, and I tried it, and then one day I had an extraordinary experience in meditation in which I felt a connectedness to All That Is in such an unbelievable way, that I would never now go very long without meditating.

So I discovered something there. It's like discovering that asparagus doesn't really taste bad after all; in fact it tastes quite, quite good, you see. So try it. Move past the edge of your comfort zone.

I'm now, by the way, trying to do this with exercise. Exercise and I have not been very good friends over the years. But I now have a little gymnasium, just a small little room in which I have a few machines in my home, and I'm trying to talk myself into going down there two or three times a week and doing a light workout. I'm sure it would do wonders for me. It's that kind of thing, it's really simple. There's no magic here, there's no mystery. Just give yourself permission to pay attention.

What is the internal guidance system?

Each of us has an internal guidance system by which we can know all there is to know about life. All that's really important to know about life. And if we will listen to that internal guidance system, we'll find ourselves led to the right and perfect people, places, and circumstances that are prepared to give us an opportunity to express the grandest part of who we are.

For me, that internal guidance system is not difficult to pay attention to. I feel it in my stomach. I often say to people: "Listen to you tummy. The tummy knows." So here's a process, here's a tool that I want to share with people, that can help them know when they're moving in the right direction, or when they're about to make a wrong decision. It's really quite simple.

First of all, get off dead center. If you find yourself in a place called, "stuck," you're neither doing this nor that, or shrinking from the decision for fear of making a wrong choice, make some choice. Make any choice. Step toward something.

I always advise people to do that, just move into the process called "decision making," and step toward something. As soon as you definitely decide to do or not do a thing, to choose or not choose a thing, as soon as you move in one particular direction or another, within moments your tummy will tell you whether or not that's the place you should go. It's an internal guidance system. For me it's in my stomach; for others it's located maybe as a thought in their head. But all of us have that internal guidance system.

You can tell when you're up to something that your whole system is rebelling against and saying, "No, don't do that." And that is not fear. It's a feeling of inner wisdom saying: "I don't really think so. I don't really think you want to do this." Or, an inner knowing that says: "Yes, this, this is the right move. Go, go, go." There's a sense of joy, a *joie de vivre*. The soul is saying: "I'm with you on this. Let's go, let's go for it." And that's an inner feeling, but it comes to you only *after* you've made a decision, not before. And people are often waiting to get that feeling, that guidance, before they make a decision.

Now this is a key point; I want to reiterate this, okay? I know many people who pray and meditate and ask God for guidance before they make a decision. I'm going to turn that whole thing upside down. I'm going to reverse that whole idea. People sit there and they say, "Oh God, please help me, give me guidance now, before I make this decision." And I'm going to say, "No, no, no; make the decision one way or the other, then listen to the guidance that you're receiving from every cell of your body."

See, it's just the reverse. Don't be afraid of the choice. Make the choice, then you'll know whether you've made the right one. And if it feels wrong to you, stop, turn around, and go back. And if it feels right to you, keep on going. Isn't that an interesting idea?

Neale, I have a couple more questions about the body, primarily regarding suffering. Would you equate a breakdown in the physical body to do with something on a soul level that needs to be healed? You know, metaphysically, they say that if you have a cold, you're confused—that kind of thing. And the other question that I had was about people who are physically in pain, and their spiritual journey. Is it possible for people who are suffering physically to really have this awakening experience when they're in pain, when they're suffering?

Well, the Buddhists say all of life is suffering. And within that context, the answer is clearly yes. Suffering is. Suffering is experience. I mean, what *you* might call suffering, I might not. For instance, I'm a chronic pain patient. There are very few moments of the day when I'm not in pain. I've been in pain throughout this entire presentation. And yet, really, relative to moments when I'm really in pain, I'm not in pain. Can you understand what I'm saying? And somebody who tells you this about me might say: "How does he do that? If I had that pain right now in my body, I wouldn't be able to begin to think straight, much less give this presentation."

I'm not trying to pat myself on the back here. I'm just telling you how it is. And that's how it is with all of us. We all have the same experience here. So, first of all, pain is a relative experience.

To some degree, almost all of us are in pain all the time. When the Buddhists said it, they meant it. Life is pain. (laugh)

Because as soon as you find yourself . . . just the very nature of our enclosure in this physical form, really, at some level, is limiting to that degree, given that limitation is a truncation of who you really are, and is, at some level, painful. So, I don't want to skirt away from your question, but just to contextualize it a bit.

Now, to more directly address your question, yes, a person who is in pain can have moments of enormous enlightenment, and great spiritual awareness. And sometimes it's the pain that drives them to that. Because physical pain tends to shift our ideas of what's important. And we tend to focus on what's really so, and who we really are.

I remember a time I used to work on the staff of a woman named Elisabeth Kübler-Ross. Does anybody know who she is? Well, I had the pleasure of working with Elisabeth on her staff for a blessed period of my life. And I remember once we went to visit—we often went to visit—the homes of the terminally ill. It was a great education. You know, if you really want to have an education, go to the homes of ten dying people in a week. And that's not something that the average person will have the opportunity to do in their lifetime. Perhaps a nurse might, or a doctor, but ordinary people might not have that opportunity.

And I remember one night, we visited this woman who was dying, and she was losing all movement and feeling in her body gradually, from the feet up. It was kind of a degenerative thing. And it would get higher. And every time we went to visit her, more of her functions were lost. Until one day she even lost the functioning of her hand. But she lost it in the moment that she was holding her little granddaughter, who was just a few weeks old. She realized that she couldn't quite move her hand any more, in the way she used to be able to. So, she had to say, you know, "I don't think I should hold the baby any more, because I don't feel so confident in my ability to hang on to the baby when she squirms."

But here's what she shared with us about that. Elisabeth said, "How did that feel for you to lose that feeling in your hand? How does that feel?" She was asking her to probe her experience. And the woman said, with the most benign look on her face, "You know, the first time I—the moment I realized that my hand didn't work quite as well as it used to was when I was watching this little eight-week-old angel holding up her hand . . . and delighting in how that all worked." And she said, "To me, it was just like transferring that life from hand to hand."

Now, I'm not saying that that's the way it really is, but that she could find that metaphor in that pain is an example, absolutely, of what I'm talking about. That the level of her incapacitation, and the pain that went with it, drove her to the edge of a realization she may never otherwise have articulated as long as she lived. But she saw something spiritually significant in that moment of what we would call loss. So, is it possible that people in great pain have great insight? I think it is, and I think it's, frankly, rather common.

But you had another question in front of that, which I've completely forgotten.

I was asking about, like, the metaphysical equivalence of what's breaking down in your body. Is there something on a soul level that needs to be healed?

I think, given God's statement to me that all illness is self-created, I believe that that's true. But I don't, frankly, think we should be too terribly concerned with it. And I'm not really into the books that say, "Throbbing left knee . . . selfishness." Okay. I'll be less selfish. You know, "Aching right ear . . . lack of understanding." See, there are some books out now that may or may not be accurate. I'm not putting those books down. But I'm not sure that it serves us to get all caught up in that kind of cause-and-effect relationship, because then we can beat ourselves up. "If I only hadn't been so this and this, then my ear wouldn't be hurting quite so much. Let me try to be more understanding in order to heal the ear." You see? Or "If I can be more of this, and less of what I used to be, then I'll heal my spleen."

I think the cause-and-effect relationship, while it may be there the way that some of those books indicate, I believe, and I've been told, that it is far more subtle than that. It's very, very subtle, and could have taken place thirty or forty years ago. The original thought, the Sponsoring Thought that produced that inoperable spleen when you're forty-five, could have been a long time ago in a far more subtle way than that of which we are currently aware.

What then is our appropriate response? Love it. Accept it. What you resist, persists. Just move into the acceptance of it, and say, "This is what's happening to me now. My spleen isn't operating. I choose to accept and to bless—bless, bless, *bless* the condition, and don't condemn it. And allow the condition to simply be what it is.

And in that way, in many cases, you'll actually eliminate the condition itself. Because what you resist, persists, and what you own, you can choose to uncreate. But even if what you are owning is not uncreatable, because it's been there too long or the effects are too huge, and it's simply not going to go away; what you can uncreate, and this is profoundly true, is the *negative impact or effect* that it might have on your life. And that's what the lady did with the hand, you see. She saw the blessing in what could have been a tragedy.

I watched a master, whom I knew a little bit in the last few years of his life—I watched him die. I watched him in the last few weeks and months of his life. And this guy was dying a death that other people—again, here we go—other people would have found very painful, very inconvenient, very lacking in dignity. You know, with the catheter and the whole thing. And yet this master was teaching all those who were coming in to see him every day. Four, five, six, and eight students a day were coming to see this guy die. And you had to get an appointment to see this guy die. He was laughing about it. "You know, I'm busier now than I was when I was totally healthy."

And he knew, as did—God bless him— Joseph Cardinal Bernadine of Chicago. See, Cardinal Bernadine knew: "There's one more gift I have to give. In a life filled with the giving of the gifts of who I am, here's one more yet that I have to give. Even my death will be an affirmation of life. Even my going will be an affirmation of the great arrival. Even my pain will be an affirmation of life's grandest joy."

This guy was a master, and I learned from him about graceful dying. And he was able to teach me that, because, while he could not set aside the effects on his body of the prior decisions of his life, *he had no need to*. Because the effects on his body had nothing to do with any effect on his mind.

And when you'd say, "Are you in discomfort?" he would often look at you and say, "Oh, just a little." And you'd say, "How brave, how stoic." In truth, he was not lying. He was really in a little discomfort, whereas I might have been in a great deal of discomfort with the same experience. Because he had moved to a place of mastery, and he very rarely allowed the physical experiences of his life to dictate who he was in that moment. That's very powerful stuff. And we've all known people who have died with such grace. And not only with dignity, but with such a gift for others.

I'll tell you a final story about someone who died like that. My mother was a saint. Everybody's mother was a saint, but my mother was the original saint mother of all time. She really was. And I remember the day that she died, the moment that she died, very clearly. As she was moving into her final moments, they called the priest from the local parish. And he was a young guy. They rushed in there, and this guy couldn't have been nineteen-and-a-half years old. I'm not sure that he really shaved yet. But there he was, just out of the seminary. And it was very clear to all of us that this was the first time he had ever administered the last rights of the most holy Roman Catholic Church, because he was fidgeting with his scapular, and all of the oils, and the things that they do, and the things of ritual. And not to make fun of them, because ritual is very important in our collective experience. Be clear about that. Ritual has a hugely important place for all of us. But he had never done this particular ritual with a real-live, dying person. And there he was, going to go into my mother's room. And he went into my mother's room in the unit—what do they call it? Intensive care unit—and a few moments later—ten, fifteen minutes later—he came out white as a ghost. I said: "What? What? What happened?"

He said: "Well, I didn't know if I was doing this all right. And I was getting the wrong oil, and I was trying to get it straight. And your mother looked at me, and said: 'Father, relax. There's no way you can make a mistake here.' She said, 'It's your intention. It's what you bring to the moment. It's your thought that counts, not what you're doing.'" And he looked at me, and tears filled his eyes. He said, "Your mother was comforting me as she died."

And so I will share with you that death need not be a tragedy. And I only hope that when I die, it can hold even a little bit of that grace. And just a tiny particle of that kind of wisdom.

You know, I have a question about the agenda of the soul. In reference to the idea that on some other plane, we—plan the places, and things, and people that we're going to be involved with in this life. I'd just like to know . . . can you comment on that in terms of the idea of why there are no accidents. Is it because we've already planned this on some level?

Yes. Well, I've been told that we do have an agenda when we come into the body, and that it's a shared agenda. And, in fact, I want to let all of you know that none of us are here in this room by accident. All of us decided to be here at this time and place, at some very, very high level. Then we might notice, once again, and support each other in being who we really are.

And here we have come. We have a compact, we have an agreement, and we are fulfilling our parts of that agreement, even as we interact in the way we are interacting on this very day.

That's true, by the way, of people who are being kind to each other, and people who are being unkind to each other. True saintliness and true mastery is noticing that there are no victims and there are no villains, and that the person who is persecuting you is merely playing out an agreement made at a whole different level, so that you might express and experience— announce, declare, become, and then fulfill Who You Really Are. That's why all masters have said, "Judge not, and neither condemn."

And so, yes, we are each of us embarked on journeys that we call this life. And it is a journey, a destination—the destination we have already determined, but not how we're going to get there. Nor is it guaranteed that we will, in fact, arrive at that destination. We simply have an idea of where we would like to go, and what we would like to do. But there is no predestination in the sense that we are guaranteed of arriving there, nor is there any guarantee that the way we get there will be accurately followed.

With each incoming opportunity we have a chance to move forward with our agenda. If we don't move forward with that agenda, we will, in fact, create other continuing opportunities until we do move forward with that agenda. Anybody ever see repeating patterns in your life? So you'll just keep on doing it, and doing it, and doing it until you get it right. You'll keep on bringing in the same person five times.

Did you hear what I said? I married the same person five times in five different bodies—until I finally got what I was supposed to get about that. And then I was able, finally, to not marry that person any more. And so, too, has it been with other people and events in my life. Confronting the same kinds of events over and over again, until I didn't anymore; until I finally got what that means. So, we'll pattern it out, and we'll bring into our experience exactly the kinds of people, places, and events we need to bring in, in order to produce the outcomes that our agenda calls for. And it may not all be complete in this lifetime. In fact, I would be surprised if it were. But it is of no matter, because you'll have another lifetime, and another, and another still, and even more until the end of time, which has no end at all. And so it will just continue, and go on, and on, and on, forever, and even forevermore. Isn't that delicious?

In Book 3, *God talks about highly evolved beings. Should we be trying to operate that way?*

There are such things in the universe as highly evolved beings. I refer to them in my own little shorthand as "HEBs," Highly Evolved Beings. And these beings have learned how to coexist with nature and the universe around them joyfully and harmoniously. And they've learned how to live lives that are largely pain-free and struggle-free, and here's how they've done it. It's a two-part formula. And it's a two-part formula that we could apply right here on this planet, if we chose to.

These people currently live off the planet, largely. I have not observed a large number of highly evolved beings on this planet (with the possible exception of those who walk the halls of Congress).

That was a joke.

Here's how highly evolved beings operate. They function on a very simple two-part system. Part one: They observe what's so, and say it. That's part one. In other words, to be simple about it, I observe what's so. You're sitting there in a chair. And we're talking together. Or I observe what's so: television is full of violence. And children spend a lot of time watching television, and then children act out that violent behavior. That's just what's so. Or, tobacco can cause cancer. And because it can cause cancer, it probably isn't the healthiest thing in the world to ingest it or to smoke. That's just what's so. So I observe what's so and then I say it. That is to say, I tell the truth about it.

On this planet, most people who observe what's so refuse to announce what they're seeing. In fact, they sometimes say the opposite of what they're seeing, for fear of offending someone or revealing something about themselves that they don't want anyone to know. So, on this planet we observe what's so and then we lie about it. That's a behavior that's common among most people, and very common in our institutions of politics and religion and so forth.

If it doesn't work in highly evolved societies for their offspring to act in violent ways,

then they do what works and remove violent in-
fluences from the children during their
formative years. Therefore, in a highly evolved
society, it would be unheard of to place them in
front of little square boxes for four to eight
hours a day and expose them to the very kinds
of behaviors that we are asking them not to ex-
hibit. You see, it's really quite simple. It's so
simple, it's almost laughable.

In our society, we're doing an amazing
number of things that don't work. And it isn't
because we don't know that they don't work.
The insanity of it is that we are clear that they
don't work, and we're doing them anyway.
That's the insanity of it. We're clear that they
don't work, and we're doing them anyway. Example: we know that it doesn't work to put
children in front of that box for several hours a
day, exhibiting violent behavior, and expect
children not to reflect that behavior. We know
that doesn't work and we do it anyway.

We know that it doesn't work to pour huge
amounts of money from special interests into
our political system, and expect our political

system to work without bias. We know that doesn't work and we do it anyway.

We know that it doesn't work to consume huge amounts of red meat every day of our lives and expect our bodies to react in a way that's healthy. We know that that doesn't work, and we do it anyway. We know, in advance, that it doesn't work to ingest smoke and carcinogens into our system, and yet we do it anyway. And I'm only listing four or five examples. I can give you hundreds of examples like that—probably, if I thought about it, thousands.

Now, the intelligent being has to ask, why? Why would we continue to do these things that we know simply don't work? And the answer is: I don't think that we have the courage of our convictions. I think that we're more comfortable saying one thing and doing another. I don't think that we're truly committed to expressing the highest version of who we really are. I think that we're very immature beings.

As sentient beings in the universe go, we're really rather primitive. We simply don't have the willpower to make the highest choice. But we're getting there. We're starting to change. We're seeing some shifting with regard to that, as more and more people are questioning these things that I am talking about. And we're now seeing some spiritual and moral leadership at last on the planet, where we are able to stand up and say, in larger numbers, at last: "Hey, this doesn't work. This simply isn't working." So why don't we do an interesting thing: Why don't we just stop it?

Would you speak please to the role of women and, beyond that, the feminine into the new millennium?

Well, uh—that's a huge topic. And I'm not sure exactly what it is you want me to say about that. I will make this comment, from what I understand and know. At one point in our history, on this planet, we were largely dominated in our society's power structures by what I'm going to call feminine energy. During the period of the matriarchy, it was the female of the species who made the decisions, and ran the institutions, and had things largely their way. And that went on, not for a short period of time, but for a rather long period of time. And then, after several thousand years of that, there was kind of a shift in the paradigm, and we wound up with what I'm going to call the patriarchy, where men have largely had their way, and have run the institutions, and have created the places of power and so forth. In each of those paradigms, it was a process of either one or the other.

And now what's happening, as we move into the new millennium, is that we're seeing this third paradigm, the one for which we've all yearned lo these many thousands of years—a new construction and a new paradigm, in which male and female find themselves conjoined, and in which the roles that traditionally separated men from women are no longer (thank goodness) clearly defined or, specifically assigned, by gender.

Power is shared, and will be increasingly shared between men and women in the years just ahead of us now, as we march headlong into the twenty-first century. And we'll find more and more women (thank goodness) moving into places of influence, power, and authority, of creativity, and of impact in our society throughout the world.

We're beginning to see it now, and the day will come when we'll have, as I mentioned in an earlier conversation, a female president, a female pope (if you please), and females in all of the heretofore male-only positions within human society. And blessed be the day. And then we will have both men and women, almost at random, holding these kinds of positions. And we'll find ourselves blessed for that, because there will truly be a balance struck.

This is a balance we've been seeking for a very, very long time. And in the overall scheme of things, in the history of the universe (the universal level), this balance has been struck relatively quickly.

You know, several thousand years is relatively quickly in the billion-year history of the universe. So rather quickly *Homo sapiens* have been here, and been there, and now they're beginning to strike a balance. Although in our particular experience of it, it feels like it's taking a very, very long time, it's really just a blink of an eye, just a whisper in the life of the universe. And so we've now found, or are beginning to find, this place of balance. And we're seeing it in politics. We're seeing it in our corporations. We're seeing it, really, all over. I'm delighted to see, as I get on airplanes all over America, flight attendants that are male. What used to be a totally female thing to do, for reasons that were never really clear to me, we're seeing males now do.

I have a dentist who is a female, and she's a wonderful dentist. And when I was five, and even ten years old, I don't think you found one female dentist out of a thousand. And so we're starting to see this cross-occupational, cross-gender change, and so forth. And one day we might even allow ourselves to have female priests. Wouldn't it be nice to have, even in the orthodox churches, female rabbis and female ministers?

Soon, we'll begin to share those places of power in the most revered of our institutions: in our religions, in our politics, and in other positions of influence. And as I said, blessed be the day. Because we have been living half a life.

God knows, men haven't done a very good job of running this planet for these past several thousand years. We have not been very effective. And we need that kind of balancing, feminine energy of insight, and patience, and compassion, and deep awareness, and extraordinary sensitivity to the human experience. It's part of the female experience, and of the feminine energy, in all of us. And I hope we'll nurture it, and continue to allow it to flourish as a portion of the largest measure of who we are.

How did you discover who you were?

For the largest number of the Earth's people, day-to-day survival is no longer the primary focus. It is for some—too many, frankly—but it is not for the largest number any more. So now what is the primary focus? The

key question before the human race now, therefore, is not how will I survive, but who is it that
is surviving? I mean, who am I? *Who am I?* The
thinking person seeks to know, begs to know.
That is not an empty question. It's an important
question, because most people have no idea
who they are. I mean, I didn't have any idea
who I was until very, very recently.

You know, when I was sixteen years old, I
thought I was my hair. I really did. I thought I
was my hair, and I was so clear that I was my
hair that if my hair didn't turn out just right in
the morning, I would throw the brush into the
sink and refuse to be seen in public because no
one would know who I am, you see.

Actually, not much has changed through
the years. I sometimes still wake up in the
morning thinking, you know, I'm my hair.

But when I turned eighteen, I realized that I
was not my hair. I came to my eighteenth year
filled with the wisdom of that time of my life.
And I said to myself: "Isn't it crazy that I once
actually thought, I'm my hair? Of course I'm
not my hair." At eighteen, I knew the truth. I'm

my car. I *knew* that I was my car, because I could sense other kids having ideas about me, thoughts about me, based on what car I was driving. Once, my car wasn't working, and my father said to me: "Well here, take my car tonight. You can have the car for the evening."

I said: "Are you crazy? I wouldn't be caught dead in your car." I mean no one would know *who I was*.

My father drove an Oldsmobile.

Today I drive an Oldsmobile.

And the sins of the father *shall* be visited upon the sons.

But when I turned twenty-one, I grew out of all of that. And at twenty-one, great wisdom befell me. And I realized: "Wait a minute, I'm not my hair. I'm not my car. This is crazy, of course." At twenty-one I knew the truth. I'm my women.

And I want you to know that I played the game called "I am my women" for a very long time. It was a delicious game to play. And I *knew* that I was my women. I could feel the thoughts of people around me in the room. I could feel my *own* thoughts, my own ideas about myself change, depending on who I did have, or who I did not have, on my arm.

So I lived "I am my women" for a very long time. And then I thought, one day as I woke up, "Wait a minute, I can't be my women, because if I'm my women, I must have multiple personality disorder." You see, because there were so many of them. So, I realized that there must be something larger than this, that I am. Who am I? Who am I? The mind begs to know.

And then I got clear. Oh, I must have been in my late thirties or very early forties. And suddenly it dawned on me, of course, and I know the time it happened, because my father made a point of it. He said, the kid's finally grown up. Because I decided, and all of my actions from that point on indicated, that I am my job, as many men at that point in their lives, and some women too, conclude. And boy, I played that game full out. I'm my job. I mean, you know how it looked in my life? It looked like hey, hey, hey, it's my job; it's my work; I have to, I have no choice; this is my work.

Then I woke up to that unreality as well. I looked at myself one day and I said: "Wait a minute. I can't be my job. I've been fired seven times. So who am I? Who am I? If I'm not my job . . . "

Then, finally, came the answer. "Of course I'm not my women or my work, or, I'm not my car. I'm my family. See?" Now my *mother* said, "He's finally grown up." Because I came to my senses. I rearranged my values. And I played the game called "I am my family." I'm my children and my spouse and my loved ones. That's who I am. And I played that game full out, as well.

And what that looked like was, I didn't take a job in another community, I recall it well, because it wasn't going to be good for my family. I even refused to buy a home that I loved that was just a few blocks away, but it was in the wrong school district. And so I made huge life choices, you see, major decisions in life, based on the idea, I am my family.

Then, one day I came home from a job that I despised, from the life of quiet desperation that I was leading, opened the door to my house and found that the house was totally empty—not just of people, but of furniture.

Now, you know something's amiss; I recall the moment very well. This is a true story, by the way. I'm not making this up. And I recall the moment as if it were yesterday. I opened the door. The place is empty. And my first thought was, "My God, we've been robbed." But nobody comes into your house in the middle of the day and takes all the furniture out of the place. Besides, not all the furniture was gone. I looked around and I—I saw, there in the corner, an old hi-fi set that I had brought into the marriage, and there was a coffee table that I brought with me as well, from my old bachelor pad days. And a few of my other . . . my other things were lying around, and I realized that only some of the furniture was gone.

Then it dawned on me what had happened. But I still didn't believe it. I raced upstairs to the master bedroom, you know, and I threw open her side of the closet. All of her clothes were gone. Threw open my side of the closet. All of my clothes were still there. That's when I knew the awful truth. The robber was a woman.

See, it's amazing what the mind will do to stop you from looking at what's right in front of your face. I couldn't laugh about it any more. I went downstairs and sat there on the carpet of the nearly empty living room, and I cried. "My God, what do you want with me? And who am I?"

See, I thought I was all this. I thought I was all this stuff. And now all this stuff was gone. Who am I? The eternal cry of the human soul. Who am I?

And, the answer is not outside of us. Obviously, it's not in the people and the places and the things of life. The answer resides within. And that's the whole message of *Conversations with God*.

I wanted to say, first of all, I really enjoyed reading all three books. They're pretty amazing. And my question is about the idea of the soul. It is on a journey of evolution versus the idea that if it's completely absorbed into the absolute, that there's no more evolution that takes place. What you're speaking of seems to be an expansion of the journey that becomes richer, more dynamic. The vistas are wider. And the idea that you're speaking of . . . the existence of the possibility of transcending that and stepping out of existence, or what we call the process of evolution . . . So I wonder if you'd speak of that.

You can't step out of the process of evolution. That is literally impossible. The moment you step out completely of the process of evolution, you step out completely of God, since God is a process. God is not a being; God is a process.

God is the process of life itself that we call evolution. And since it's not possible to step completely out of God, it's not possible to step completely out of evolution. Therefore, our evolution, that is to say the evolution of the lot of us, which is God, the Divine Collective, never ends. It always was, is now, and always will be, world without end. Amen.

I want to say to all of you, what a joy, and what a delight it has been to share these moments with you. How good it has been to be here in this same time and place with you. And I invite and encourage you now to go from this place and touch the world with the deepest truth that resides and abides within you. And cause everyone to know who they really are. Give them back to themselves, and let us create together the world of our grandest vision.

Bléssed be.

In Closing...

What I have learned about life is that when we live wholly, we live holy. I have been searching for ways to live my life as a whole person, as an integrated being, for twenty-five years. The first thing I came to understand about that is that, if I am to live an integrated life, I must become far more integrated with my environment. That is, I must become one with it, and treat it as if it were a part of me, not something from which I was separate, and which was separate from me.

Holistic living means being aware that I am part of a *whole system*, a *whole idea*, a *whole reality*, and that everything I think, say, and do affects that reality; indeed, at some level, creates it. I can no longer pretend that one thing has nothing to do with another. That smoking, for instance, or consuming red meat at every meal, has nothing to do with my health. That the quality of the air around me, for example, has nothing to do with the quality of my life. That how I think and speak and act has nothing to do with how I experience my future. That the way in which I interact with my environment has nothing to do with how long I will be allowed, and able, to do so.

That is how I lived before I understood what *holistic* meant. I did not understand what sociologists call Whole Systems Theory. I did not comprehend the implications of the fact that I was a cog in a very big wheel. In this, I dare say that I was not unlike many people. Perhaps, most people.

Even today, the increase in our general level of awareness notwithstanding, there appears to be a huge disconnect for many people between in-the-moment choices, decisions, and actions, and down-the-road effects. Yet living holistically is about taking into account all of our down-the-road effects. It is about becoming One with our God, with our environment, with our fellow travelers on this extraordinary journey, and with our very own selves.

So many of us are not integrated. That is, we are *dis*integrated. Falling apart. Falling to pieces. And so is the environment in which we are living our disintegrated lives.

Now, at last, we are at least becoming aware of our condition. And many of us are opting out, choosing again, and recreating ourselves anew in the next grandest version of the greatest vision ever we held about Who We Are. I would like to share with you here some resources that I believe may be wonderfully useful as we undertake the process of rebuilding our collective reality in the twenty-first century.

I would direct you to the Institute of Ecolonomics, the inspiration and the work of Dennis Weaver. Dennis coined the word *ecolonomics* as a melding of ecology and economics, and it is his thought that one of the things that is needed on the planet right now is a new way of growing our economy that preserves and protects our ecology, and a new way of protecting our ecology that preserves and grows our economy.

As is true in all areas of life's whole system, we cannot act in one area without impacting the other—although we have been pretending that we can for many years now.

Dennis's dream, and the dreams of thousands across the country and around the world who are now joining with him, is to see *ecolonomics* become a new way of life; to see it actually taught in our schools as a legitimate academic subject. (In fact, several colleges have become so excited about Dennis's work that they are now designing courses in *ecolonomics*. Soon, full-fledged degrees in *ecolonomics* will be offered.)

In the meantime, public education, sharing and publicizing of leading-edge initiatives, and the engagement of leaders from business, industry, and the environmental movement in cooperative ventures, is high on the agenda for the institute. If you would like to learn more about how you may assist Dennis Weaver (and his friend, the Earth), you may make a connection at:

The Institute of Ecolonomics
Post Office Box 257
Ridgway, Colorado 81432

Even as we make friends with our environment, we must make friends with each other. We have got to find a way to get over our differences, recognize our interconnectedness, and understand that the Whole System will not work if the individuals who comprise it are not even talking to each other.

Because I know this, I am excited about the work of the Ashland Institute, part of an emerging web of practitioners who are discovering "dialogue" as a spiritual practice. Dialogue is a way of being together that sheds light on the powerful Sponsoring Thoughts that *Conversations with God* describes as guiding our society.

As the Ashland Institute uses the term, "dialogue" describes a specific process that surfaces the tensions of polarities, contradictions, and paradoxes that fill our human experience, opening a gateway to a more profound flow of meaning, in which the seeming brokenness in the world can be held—and healed.

The institute asks, through its work, a number of profound questions. What if our population was seasoned by small, dedicated circles in which people peel back the structures and reconceptions by which they define themselves? What if God could walk and talk among friends through the quality of our sensing and the origin of our words? What if dialogue were not "uncommon," but common, because we have learned how to truly listen—behind words and appearances—to ourselves, to one another, and to what life itself wants to express?

CWG says that the dialogue with God never ends. The practice of dialogue is the embodiment of a fresh-flowing river that we are always in. But our human experience, for the most part, seems parched and separate; habitual rigidities of belief and hardness of heart make us oblivious to the thirst-quenching currents we swim in, day in and day out. The Ashland Institute was created as a "remembering place," assisting people to experience the river again.

The founders of the institute have organized and participated in many informal circles of friends who have met regularly for years now, honing collective capacity to ponder the things that matter to us most; creating the experience of community so many of us dream of. They have helped many organizations and corporations develop leadership circles in which the roots of complex issues can be addressed, and old models of "command and control leadership" give way to the wisdom of collective vision.

They've sat with courageous men and women in their forties, fifties, sixties, and seventies coming to terms with grief, redefining aging, discovering the truth of eldership, and finding new relationship with death. They've convened dialogues at the request of ministers and clergy, meeting in private council to address divisive, highly personal dilemmas around homosexuality and the church. They've entered into dialogues between people of many and varying spiritual traditions, helping to create a shift from reliance on singular inspirational focus, toward honoring and coordinating the mature perceptions of many. They've gathered couples meeting with other couples, building an essential field in which evolving relationships can clarify and rest.

We are talking here about the practices of deep listening, letting go of mind-sets, filling in damaged places of the heart, embracing diversity, collective prayer, profound respect for the natural world, artistic expression, and reacquaintance with the power to create on behalf of life itself. The subject matter of the dialogues varies, but the process always provides a portal through which God may speak. For more information on this emerging work, contact:

The Ashland Institute
P.O. Box 366
Ashland, OR 97520
tel:1-541-488-0003.
e-mail: tai@mind.net

In a holistic life, even as we make friends with our environment and the people in it, we must make friends with ourselves. We must "come from" a new state of being, a new clarity about who we are and who we choose to be, and a new determination to demonstrate that in the world. When a high state of beingness is turned into doingness in the physical world, struggle disappears from our lives. We have integrated our inner and outer selves.

After I read about this in the *Conversations with God* books, I yearned to know, in a practical sense, how to achieve it; how to transform my activity in the work-a-day world into a sacred expression of Who I Really Am. The result was an inspiration to produce a small book, called *Bringers of the Light*, which those who have read it have told me has brought understanding, at last, to this mystery of life.

This little book is available from ReCreation, the non-profit foundation that Nancy and I formed a few years ago to help handle all the incoming energy (now almost 300 letters a week from all over the world) that has resulted from the publication of *Conversations with God*, and to spread its message.

If you are looking for a more interactive process, each year the foundation presents three five-day intensives, "Recreating Your Self." Based on the messages in *CWG*, they are designed especially for those who are looking closely at the lives they are currently experiencing, and seeking ways that they can bring about real change, and live life more holistically.

For more information on these retreats, write:

CWG Recreating Your Self Retreats
ReCreation Foundation
PMB #1150
1257 Siskiyou Blvd.
Ashland, OR 97520

In addition, many questions on holistic living—and, for that matter, all of the issues covered in the *Conversations with God* material—are addressed in the regular newsletter of the foundation. (We named the foundation ReCreation because of the message of CWG that the purpose of life is to recreate yourself anew in the next grandest version of the greatest vision ever you held about Who You Are.) The newsletter contains questions from readers everywhere on how to do just that. I answer each letter personally.

If you would like to "stay connected" with the energy of CWG, you may obtain a 12-issue subscription to the letter by sending $35 ($45 for addresses outside the U.S.) to the foundation.

The last resource I want to share with you is a wonderful collection of the best of these queries and responses over the past five years, entitled *Questions and Answers on Conversations with God*. It and the *CWG Guidebook* (both published by Hampton Roads) are two of the most helpful books ever produced for those who truly seek to understand the *CWG* material more fully, and to find practical ways to apply it in their every day lives.

By these and other means, I hope that we can all learn more about holistic living, what it really is, and how to experience it. Once upon a time, all of us lived this way. We moved through our days and times feeling whole, living whole, and being whole. We understood ourselves to be part of a Whole System, and we did nothing individually that would negatively affect us collectively. If we can get back to that place, we can heal our lives, and heal the world.

Blessèd be.

Hampton Roads Publishing Company
publishes and distributes books on a variety of subjects,
including metaphysics, health, complementary medicine,
visionary fiction, and other related topics.

To order books or to receive a copy of our latest catalog,
call toll-free, 1-800-766-8009,
or send your name and address to:

Hampton Roads Publishing Company, Inc.
134 Burgess Lane
Charlottesville, VA 22902

email: hrpc@hrpub.com
web site: http://www.hrpub.com

*Neale Donald Walsch on Relationships, Neale Donald
Walsch on Abundance,* and *Neale Donald Walsch on Holistic Living* are based on the concepts in *Conversations with
God*, and are available on audiocassette from your local
bookstore or New World Library at 1-800-972-6657 ext. 52,
or from their website at nwlib.com.